APRIL 50 COLORING PAGES FOR ADULTS RELAXATION

SHIH CHIEN HUA

PUBLISHED BY:
SHIH CHIEN HUA
Copyright © 2018

SEABIRD SHOP >50FOR

FB FAN PAGE

Disclaimer
The information contained in this book is for general information purposes only. The information is provided by the authors and while we endeavor to keep the information up to date and correct, we make no representations or warranties of any kind, express or implied, about the completeness, accuracy, reliability, suitability or availability with respect to the book or the information, products, services, or related graphics contained in the book for any purpose. Any reliance you place on such information is therefore strictly at your own risk.

APRIL 1ST

note:

_____

_____

_____

APRIL 2ND

note:

_____

_____

_____

APRIL 3RD

note:

_____

_____

_____

APRIL 4TH

note:

_____

_____

_____

APRIL 5TH

note:

_____

_____

_____

APRIL 6TH

note:

_____

_____

_____

APRIL 7TH

note:

_____

_____

_____

APRIL 8TH

note:

_____

_____

_____

APRIL 9TH

note:

_____

_____

_____

APRIL 10TH

note:

_____

_____

_____

APRIL 11TH

note:

_____

_____

_____

APRIL 12TH

note:

_____

_____

_____

APRIL 13TH

note:

_____

_____

_____

APRIL 14TH

note:

_____

_____

_____

APRIL 15TH

note:

_____

_____

_____

APRIL 16TH

note:

_____

_____

_____

APRIL 17TH

note:

_____

_____

_____

APRIL 18TH

note:

_____

_____

_____

APRIL 19TH

note:

_____

_____

_____

APRIL 20TH

note:

_____

_____

_____

APRIL 21TH

note:

_____

_____

_____

APRIL 22TH

note:

_____

_____

_____

APRIL 23TH

note:

_____

_____

_____

APRIL 24TH

note:

_____

_____

_____

APRIL 25TH

note:

_____

_____

_____

APRIL 26TH

note:

_____

_____

_____

APRIL 27TH

note:

_____

_____

_____

APRIL 28TH

note:

_____

_____

_____

APRIL 29TH

note:

_____

_____

_____

APRIL 30TH

note:

_____

_____

_____

APRIL 31TH

note:

_____

_____

_____

APRIL 32TH

note:

_____

_____

_____

APRIL 33TH

note:

_____

_____

_____

APRIL 34TH

note:

_____

_____

_____

APRIL 35TH

note:

_____

_____

_____

APRIL 36TH

note:

_____

_____

_____

APRIL 37TH

note:

_____

_____

_____

APRIL 38TH

note:

_____

_____

_____

APRIL 39TH

note:

_____

_____

_____

APRIL 40TH

note:

_____

_____

_____

APRIL 41TH

note:

_____

_____

_____

APRIL 42TH

note:

_____

_____

_____

APRIL 43TH

note:

_____

_____

_____

APRIL 44TH

note:

_____

_____

_____

APRIL 45TH

note:

_____

_____

_____

APRIL 46TH

note:

_____

_____

_____

APRIL 47TH

note:

_____

_____

_____

APRIL 48TH

note:

_____

_____

_____

APRIL 49TH

note:

_____

_____

_____

APRIL 50TH

note:

_____

_____

_____